Thomasina Smith's Fantastic
Face Painting

southwater

This edition is published by Southwater

Distributed in the UK by
The Manning Partnership
251–253 London Road East
Batheaston
Bath BA1 7RL
tel. 01225 852 727
fax 01225 852 852

Published in the USA by
Anness Publishing Inc.
27 West 20th Street
Suite 504
New York
NY 10011
fax 212 807 6813

Distributed in Canada by
General Publishing
895 Don Mills Road
400–402 Park Centre
Toronto, Ontario M3C 1W3
tel. 416 445 3333
fax 416 445 5991

Distributed in Australia by
Sandstone Publishing
Unit 1, 360 Norton Street
Leichhardt
New South Wales 2040
tel. 02 9560 7888
fax 02 9560 7488

Southwater is an imprint of Anness Publishing Limited
Hermes House, 88–89 Blackfriars Road, London SE1 8HA
tel. 020 7401 2077; fax 020 7633 9499

© Anness Publishing Limited 1997, 2002

Publisher: Joanna Lorenz
Editor: Lyn Coutts
Photographer: John Freeman
Designer: Edward Kinsey

Previously published as *Face Painting Fun*

1 3 5 7 9 10 8 6 4 2

Introduction

Face and body painting is a tradition that goes back thousands of years. In many ancient cultures, face and body painting was used to camouflage tribespeople when they went hunting. Other societies used it as part of their religious customs.

In our society today, we use face and body painting mostly to have fun and to entertain. You can face paint yourself for special occasions, fancy dress parties, school plays or to go to a wonderful street carnival. Even putting on ordinary make-up is a form of face painting.

Face painting can transform you into someone, or even something, entirely different. With little more than a collection of face paint colors, sponges and brushes you can become a ferocious leopard, an Egyptian queen, a ghostly ghoul or even a surprise birthday present. So, go on and transform yourself, a friend or even your parents! There is no limit to the fun you can have.

Thomasina Smith

Contents

Materials and Equipment

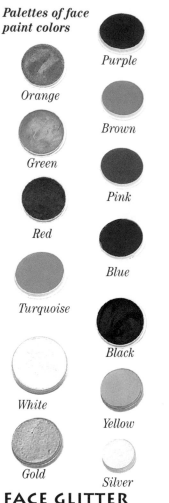

Palettes of face paint colors

Orange

Purple

Green

Brown

Red

Pink

Turquoise

Blue

White

Black

Gold

Yellow

Silver

BODY AND FACE PAINTING KIT

You can buy kits that contain all the materials you will need to do body or face painting. It is often cheaper to buy a kit than to buy equipment separately.

BOWL OF WATER

You will need a bowl of water to moisten and to wash sponges and brushes.

BRUSHES

You can buy special make-up brushes, or you can use good quality watercolor brushes. Make-up brushes are useful for painting areas that are too small for a sponge. You will need three brushes to complete the projects in this book – a fine, a medium and a thick brush.

COTTON PADS

Use these with eye make-up remover cream and face cleansers to gently remove face paint. They can be bought at drugstores and supermarkets.

EYE MAKE-UP REMOVER CREAM

This cream will remove face paint from around the eyes without stinging. It is always best to ask an adult before using any type of make-up removing product.

FACE CLEANSERS

Face paint can be washed off with mild soap and water, but proper face cleansers can be gentler on your skin. Always check with an adult before using any type of make-up remover product.

FACE PAINTS

These are available in kits or in individual palettes. Buy good quality face paints because they are easy to use, long-lasting and give a very good finish. They come in many colors, including gold and silver. You can buy face paints at specialty stores.

FACE CRAYONS

Face crayons are very inexpensive but they are not as easy to use as regular face paints.

FACE GLITTER

This glitter is specially made to be used on the face. It is available at specialty stores.

FLANNEL

An old towel is great for wiping away excess paints from your face.

GLITTER GEL

This is a clear gel make-up that contains colored glitter.

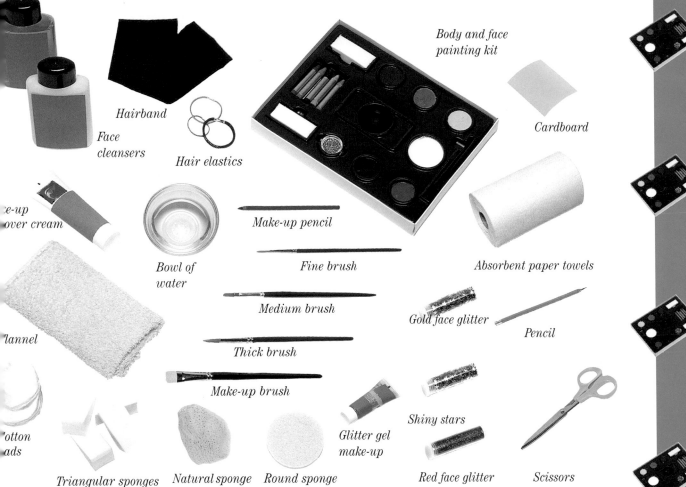

Face cleansers

Hairband

Hair elastics

Body and face painting kit

Cardboard

...e-up ...over cream

Bowl of water

Make-up pencil

Fine brush

Absorbent paper towels

...lannel

Medium brush

Gold face glitter

Pencil

Thick brush

Make-up brush

Glitter gel make-up

Shiny stars

...otton ...ads

Triangular sponges

Natural sponge

Round sponge

Red face glitter

Scissors

HAIRBAND AND HAIR ELASTICS

These are essential to prevent long hair from getting covered in face paint. They will also keep hair from smudging wet face paint.

MAKE-UP PENCIL

This is useful for painting fine lines onto the face. A sharpened face crayon or face paint applied with a fine brush can be used instead.

NATURAL SPONGE

You can buy a small, inexpensive natural sponge at drugstores and some supermarkets. The texture of this sponge makes it ideal for creating a dappled effect.

ROUND SPONGE

This smooth, round sponge is used for applying a base coat of face paint. Pre-moistened sponges are sold at drugstores in sealed plastic bags.

SHINY STARS

These tiny stars are made especially to be used on the face. They come in tubes and can be bought at specialty stores.

TRIANGULAR SPONGES

These are standard make-up sponges. It is a good idea to have two or three so you do not have to wash them every time you change face paint colors.

7

Basic Techniques

APPLYING THE BASE COLOR

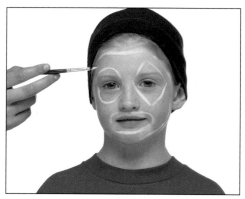

1 Use a medium or thick brush to paint the outline of a circle around the face and any other features. Paint the outlines in the base color. The instructions will always state which color should be used.

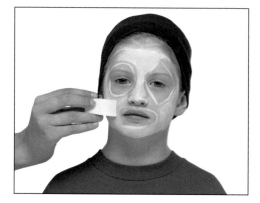

2 Dampen a round or triangular sponge in water. Rub the sponge gently around the face paint palette a few times to load sufficient color onto the sponge. Fill in the outline with base color.

3 When the outline is filled in, use a brush to neaten the edges. A brush is also useful for painting awkward areas around the nose and eyes.

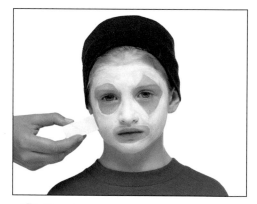

4 Use the sponge to get an even finish. In some cases, a second base coat will need to be applied to achieve this. Let the face paint dry between coats.

APPLYING A TWO-COLOR BASE

1 Outline the face using a triangular sponge or a round sponge folded in half. The instructions will always state which color to use. Do not worry if the outline is rough or uneven.

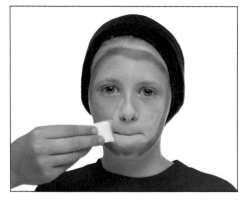

2 Use another clean sponge to apply the second color. This color will go inside the outline. It is always best to close your mouth when face paint is being applied to the lower half of your face.

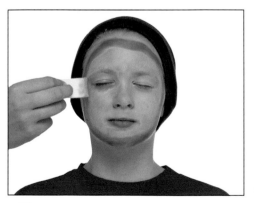

3 When face paint is being applied around your eyes, close your eyes but do not scrunch them up tightly. The face paint will not go into the creases.

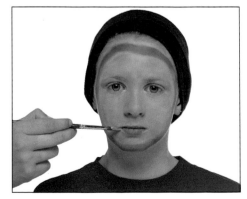

4 When the outline is filled in, use a fine or medium brush to neaten edges. Also use the brush to touch up gaps around the nose and mouth.

Painting Lips and Eyes

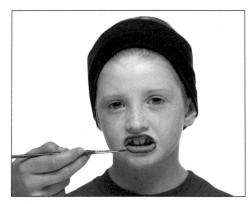

1 Outline the lips with the fine brush. It is best if you keep your lips apart when this is being done as it makes it easier to paint a smooth, even line.

2 Use a fine or medium brush to fill in the outline with face paint. Do not forget to let the paint dry before continuing with the face painting.

3 Before starting to paint, check that there are no loose bristles on the brush. You will need to close your eyes while they are being painted.

4 When paint is being applied under your eyes, look up toward the ceiling. Use a fine or medium brush and start at the inside of each eye and move outward.

Face Painting Tips

DO

1 It is best to buy proper face paints. They will be more expensive than some alternatives, but they are easier to use and give a smoother finish.

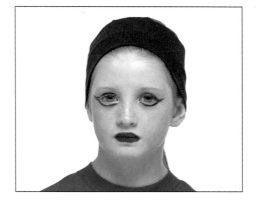

2 Though some projects may take a little while to complete, it is important that you sit as still as possible. Sit in front of a mirror so you can watch the face painting progress.

DO NOT

3 You must never use poster paints, felt tip markers, crayons, craft glues or other stationery items on your face. They may cause a rash or irritation.

4 Try not to accidentally touch wet face paint as it will smudge very badly. Even when dry, face paint will smudge if it is rubbed.

Equipment Care

1 Wash brushes in water and dry them with an absorbent paper towel. Do not leave them standing in water. Always rinse your brushes and sponges when you are changing face paint colors.

2 It is fine to mix face paint colors on the palette. To protect the paints, wash the surface of the palette under the tap. Wipe around the edge of the palette to remove excess paint.

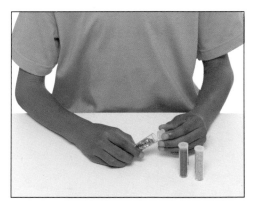

3 Always replace the lid on face painting equipment when it is not being used. This will prevent glitter from spilling and will also keep face paints moist and clean.

4 To moisten and to clean brushes and sponges, always have a medium size bowl of water nearby. The water should be changed regularly.

Removing Face Paint

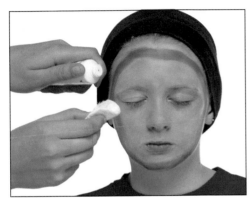

1 Tie hair back off the face. You will need to close your eyes when face paint around the eyes is being removed. Dab a cotton pad with a little eye make-up remover and rub gently.

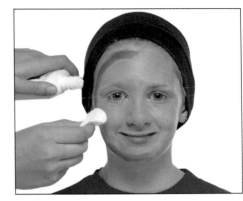

2 Use a face cleanser to remove the rest of the face paint. Check with an adult before using any type of make-up remover or cleanser. Face paint will also wash off with mild soap and water.

3 When most of the face paint has been removed you can wash off any excess with mild soap and water. There is no need to rub hard, face paints come off very easily.

4 Dry your face with a towel. Sometimes traces of face paint can be left behind, so it is best to use an old towel. Rinse out the sink when you have finished.

Spotted Puppy

There is only one thing more adorable than a puppy...a spotted puppy. The face painting for this extra-cute canine is easy to do. It is perfect for someone trying their hand at face painting for the very first time.

YOU WILL NEED

*Hairband or hair
  elastics*
*Bowl of water and
  absorbent paper towels*
*Face paints (pink, white,
  black, red)*
*Round and natural
  sponges*
Fine and thick brushes

14

1 Tie hair off the face. Use a thick brush to paint a thick ink circle around the edge of the face. Close your eyes and mouth while your face is being painted white with the round sponge.

2 Use the fine brush to paint a black circle around one eye and around the nose. Paint a black line from the base of the nose to the upper lip. Paint two black lines from the corners of the mouth to the jawline.

3 Color the nose pink using the thick brush. Paint black dots on the nose with the fine brush. Dab pink face paint on either side of the mouth with a natural sponge. The sponge will create a dappled effect.

4 Make a smile while your lips are being painted. Stretching the lips helps the face paint go on smoothly. Use the fine brush to paint the upper lip black. Then paint the lower lip red.

5 Use the fine brush to paint black dots onto the cheeks. Paint circles onto the forehead, cheeks and chin with the fine brush. Paint the circles black. Close your eyes while a line is painted onto both eyelids.

6 Paint the back of the hands with white face paint using the round sponge. Paint black lines along the tops of the fingers and outline four circles with a fine brush. Fill in the circles with black.

Soccer Hero

You do not have to buy your soccer team's uniform – you can paint it on! Body painting is lots of fun, especially when the paint is being applied to ticklish spots! Try not to laugh too much or you will end up with socks covered with wiggly lines. Remove body paint under the shower and dry yourself with an old towel.

YOU WILL NEED

Bowl of water and absorbent paper towels
Face paints (white, red, blue, black)
Fine, medium and thick brushes
Round sponge

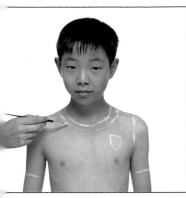

1 Make an outline in white face paint of the front and the back the soccer shirt. This is best done th a medium or thick brush. Do t forget to paint the outline of the am's badge.

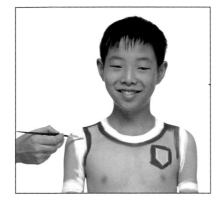

2 Use the thick brush to paint red lines inside the white outlines. Paint a red line around the waist. In white face paint, go over the outline to make the collar. Paint the sleeves white with a thick brush.

3 Use the round sponge to paint the rest of the shirt. To make the face paint go on easily, slightly moisten the sponge before applying the face paint. Paint the details on the badge using a fine brush.

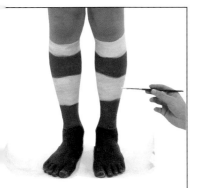

4 Wash the sponge and cover the floor with absorbent paper wels. Paint the tops of the feet ck using the clean sponge. Use a ick brush to paint red and white nds around both legs.

5 Stand as still as you can while the black paint dries. When it is dry, paint on white boot laces with a medium or thick brush. To make the laces show up, apply the white face paint thickly.

6 Paint short black lines onto the top band with a medium brush. Then paint a black line around the leg for the top of the sock. The paint must be dry before the soccer hero can kick the ball.

Sea World

Would you like to be transformed into a living marine fantasy? It is easy and lots of fun. The crab painted around your mouth will move every time you smile or talk. When you blink your eye, the fish will look as though it is moving. It is fantastic!

YOU WILL NEED

Hairband or hair elastics
Bowl of water and
  absorbent paper towels
Face paints (brown,
  turquoise, orange, yellow,
  blue, pink, red,
  green, black)
Fine and thick brushes
Triangular sponge

1 Tie the hair back. Paint a brown outline of a fish around one eye and on one cheek. Do this with a fine brush. Paint a turquoise circle around the face. Fill the circle using the sponge.

2 When the turquoise face paint is thoroughly dry, use the thick brush to paint one fish a glowing orange color and the other a bright yellow. Let dry.

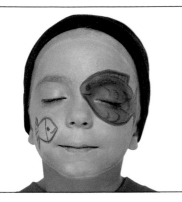

3 Paint the eyes, mouth, scales and fins onto the fish, using blue face paint and a fine brush. You must sit as still as possible while this is being done – it is tricky work!

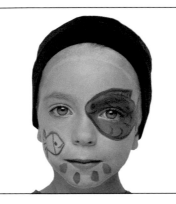

4 Break into a smile while your lips are being painted pink. Paint four pink crab claws just below the lower lip. A fine brush works best for detail work like this.

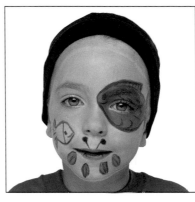

5 Use blue paint and a clean fine brush to outline and decorate the claws. Paint the face of the crab on the lower lip and draw in the legs. Paint the crab's eyes red.

6 Use the fine brush to paint wavy green fronds of seaweed onto the forehead. To make the seaweed stand out, outline it in black face paint.

Flowering Tree

This body painting of a tree is so realistic you could almost hide undetected in a tropical jungle. Even the flowers winding their way up the trunk are exotic looking. If you moved your arms as though they were branches swaying in the wind, your camouflage would be complete.

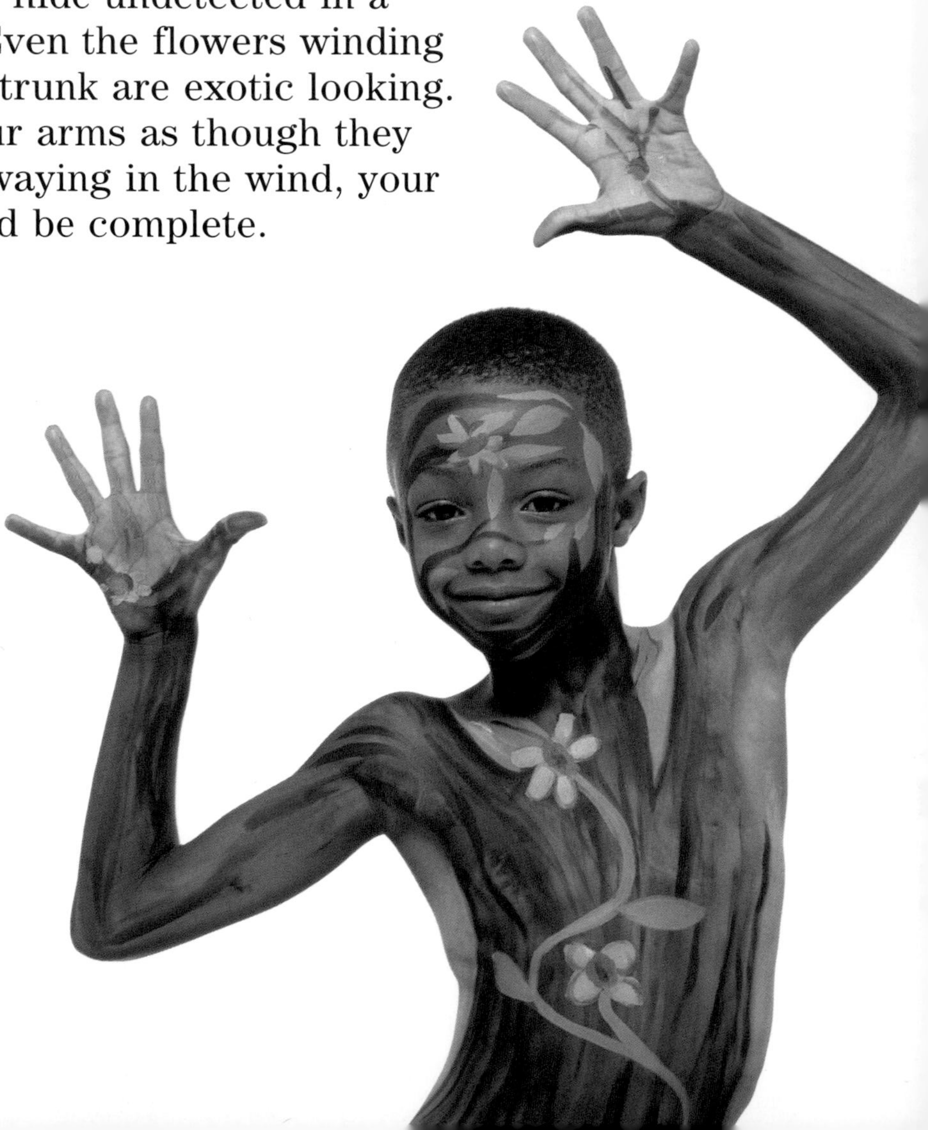

YOU WILL NEED

Hairband or hair elastics
Bowl of water and
   absorbent paper towels
Face paints (brown, red,
   yellow, green, blue, pink)
Fine, medium and thick
   brushes
Triangular sponge

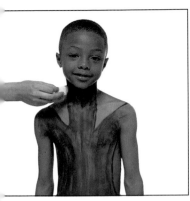

1 Tie the hair back. Use the medium brush to paint the [b]rown outline of the tree trunk onto [th]e chest and back. Use the sponge [to] fill in with brown face paint. Make [sh]ades of brown by adding red or [y]ellow to the brown face paint.

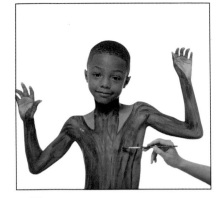

2 Paint the front and the back of the arms (the branches) in the same way. Extend the paint onto the hands but taper it to resemble the end of a branch. Outline the texture of the bark using the fine brush and brown face paint.

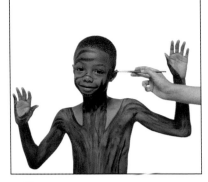

3 Use a thick brush and brown face paint to paint branches up the neck and onto the face. Make the branches twist and turn as they extend along the body. Let the paint dry thoroughly before starting the next step.

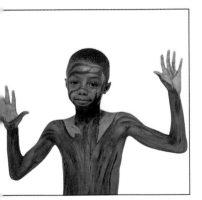

4 Wash the brush and sponge. Squeeze the sponge to get rid [o]f excess water. Draw outlines for [t]he leaves in green face paint. Fill in [t]he outlines using the thick brush.

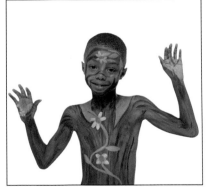

5 Paint a green stem spiraling up the trunk and linking all the leaves. Paint the flowers blue using a thick brush. When dry, paint the centers pink.

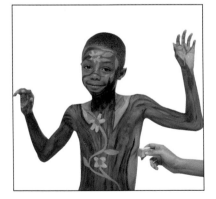

6 Use the clean sponge to paint in the background sky. This means filling in the unpainted areas with blue face paint. Apply it unevenly to look like a cloudy sky.

Puppet Doll

It is a lot of fun to make yourself up as a puppet. Traditional puppets are operated by moving the strings that are attached to their arms and legs. Because of this their movements are very jerky. Do you think you can imitate a puppet on a string?

YOU WILL NEED

Hairband or hair elastics
Bowl of water and
* absorbent paper towels*
Face paints (white, blue,
* red, black, turquoise)*
Triangular sponge
Fine, medium and thick
* brushes*
Cardboard
Pencil
Scissors

1 Tie the hair back. While your face is being painted white using the triangular sponge, close your eyes and mouth. The eyelids should not be painted white. Neaten any uneven edges with a medium brush and more white face paint.

2 Paint the eyelids blue using the thick brush. Use the fine brush to paint red circles onto the cheeks. To make the circles, cut a circle from cardboard and place it on the cheek. Paint around the circle to make the outline. Repeat for the other cheek.

3 Use the fine brush to paint on black eyebrows and long eyelashes. You will need to smile while your lips are being painted red. Use the fine brush to paint smile lines and a "cupid's bow" on the upper lip.

4 Use a medium brush to paint three parallel red lines around the neck. Then paint small red lines down the neck, as shown. Paint a red circular pendant to hang from the choker. Let dry before painting and decorating the choker and pendant with turquoise face paint.

HANDY HINT

Templates are very useful in face painting. They make it easy to paint complicated shapes and to make shapes the same size. You can make your own by tracing over pictures in books. Transfer the outline to cardboard and cut it out. Place the template onto the face or body and paint around it.

Prowling Leopard

Face painting is a great way to be transformed into an animal, especially an exotic jungle creature like the sleek, spotted leopard. To make your face look lean, mean and hungry, the outline is painted a special shape.

YOU WILL NEED

Hairband or hair elastics
Bowl of water and absorbent
*   paper towels*

Face paints (yellow, orange
*   black, red, brown)*
Fine, medium and thick
*   brushes*
Round sponge

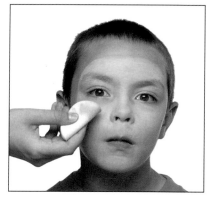

1 Tie the hair back. Paint a yellow circle around the face with a medium brush. Fill in the circle with yellow face paint applied with a round sponge. Try to apply the paint smoothly and evenly.

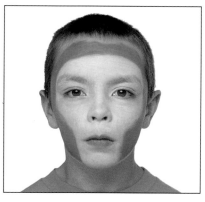

2 Use the thick brush to paint an outline around the face in orange face paint. Shape the outline as shown. Neaten the edges. Let the base color dry thoroughly before continuing.

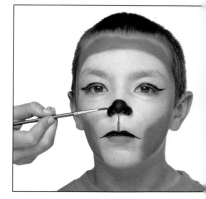

3 Close your eyes while black line are painted on your eyelids. A fine brush will be needed for this. Paint the nose and the upper lip with black face paint. Paint the line that runs from the upper lip to the nose.

4 Even leopards can smile, so their lower lip should be painted ight red. A fine brush will be needed paint the lips.

5 Use the fine brush to paint the eyebrows, spots and lines on the face brown.

6 Paint tiny brown dots below the nose with the fine brush. Paint lines from these dots to make the leopard's whiskers. Growl!

HANDY HINT

To make the leopard's ears, cut two oval shapes from orange cardboard. Fold them to make a small flap that can be taped to the forehead. Use a felt tip marker to make the marks on the ears.

Snazzy Glasses

These glasses are easy to paint and they are perfect if you do not like to wear lots of face paint. These fake glasses also let you play a great joke on your friends. When you have worn these Snazzy Glasses, create some mind-boggling designs of your own.

YOU WILL NEED

*Hairband or hair
  elastics*
*Bowl of water and
  absorbent paper towels*

*Face paints (purple, orange,
  yellow, red, green)*
Fine and medium brushes

1 Tie the hair back. Paint the outline of the glasses in purple face paint with the fine brush. Do two coats.

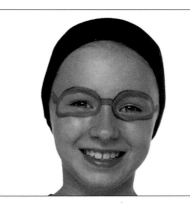

2 Make the glasses frames thicker by painting an orange line inside the purple outline. Do this with the medium brush.

3 Use the medium brush to paint the yellow wings onto the frames. The wings can be zig-zagged curvy or straight.

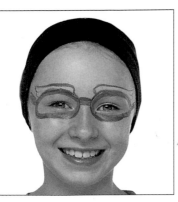

To make the crazy wings on the glasses really stand out, outline them with purple face paint. Use the fine brush for this. Do two coats, if necessary.

For a really crazy look, paint a purple and red flower on one cheek. Paint some green leaves around the flower. Apply red face paint to the lips.

27

Spooky Skeleton

This skeleton is great for Halloween trick-or-treating. The face painting is so convincing, it is truly scary. To be the best-dressed skeleton at Halloween, paint white bones onto an old black leotard or turtleneck sweater. You can make the skullcap by simply tying a black scarf tightly around your head.

YOU WILL NEED

Hairband or hair elastics
2 bowls of water and absorbent paper towels
Face paints (white, black)
Medium and thick brushes

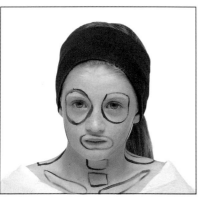

1 Tie the hair back and cover the costume with paper towels. Paint the black outlines, as shown, with a medium brush.

2 Fill in the outlines with black face paint using the thick brush. Do two coats. Let dry before starting the next step.

3 Wash the brush thoroughly. Fi in all the unpainted areas with white face paint using the clean thick brush.

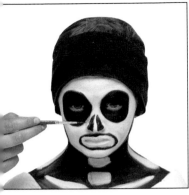

For the skeleton to be really effective, the contrast between the black and white needs to be very clear. Always wash the brush before changing colors and have separate bowls of water in which to dilute the paints.

4 Let the face paint dry. Then paint two black triangles on the nose using the fine brush. Let dry before applying a second coat of black paint.

5 Use the fine brush to paint black lines over the lips. These are the skeleton's teeth. Do a second coat to make them really white. Now it is time to rattle those bones!

29

Jewels Galore

Use face paints to make a fantastic collection of jewelry. Do it for fun or to jazz up a fancy costume. Imagine how amazed your friends will be when you turn up at a party dripping with diamonds, rubies and sapphires!

YOU WILL NEED

Hairband or hair elastics
Bowl of water and absorbent
  paper towels
Face paints (gold, red, blue, black,
  white, turquoise)
Fine and medium brushes

HANDY HINT

Gold face paint is a little more
expensive than other colors. If
you do not have gold face paint,
use yellow instead.

1 Tie the hair back. Paint the outlines of the necklace in gold face paint using a medium brush. Do two coats, if necessary.

2 Fill in the dazzling pendants and stunning gems with red and blue face paints. Use a fine or medium brush to do this.

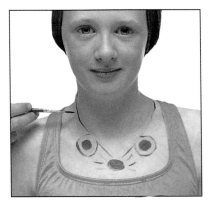

3 To make the gold stand out, paint a thin black line around the necklace and pendants with a fine brush.

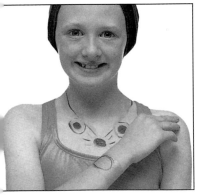

4 Paint a gold band around the wrist with the medium brush. Clean the brush. Paint the outline for the watch face with black face paint using the medium brush.

5 Paint the face of the watch white using the fine brush. Let dry and then paint the watch hands turquoise. Outline the watch strap with two black lines.

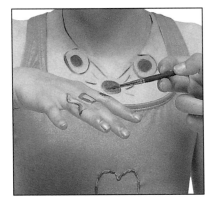

6 Use a clean fine brush to paint the gold outlines of rings onto the fingers. Let dry before painting exquisite turquoise stones onto the rings.

Munching Mouse

Mice are famous nibblers, so this field mouse has a pair of big front teeth. To play the part of a mouse you must twitch your nose, have startled-looking eyes and scurry around quickly and quietly. Practice these mousy actions and you will have friends and family clambering onto chairs!

YOU WILL NEED
Hairband or hair elastics
Bowl of water and
*   absorbent paper towels*

Face paints (white,
*   purple, black, pink)*
Fine and thick brushes

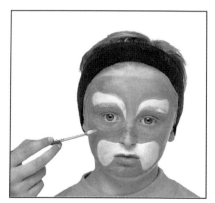

1 Tie the hair back. Paint in white eyebrows and cheeks with the thick brush. Apply the purple face paint with the thick brush.

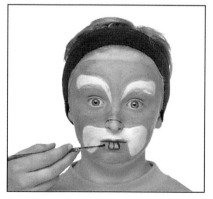

2 Use the fine brush to paint a black line over the nose. Use the same brush to paint black outlines for the teeth onto the lips.

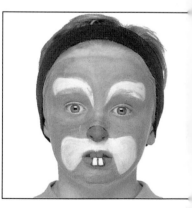

3 Paint the nose pink. Use the fine brush to paint the rest of the lips pink. Do this carefully so the teeth are not smudged.

Paint small black dots onto either side of the nose using tip of the fine brush. Paint skers sprouting from the dots.

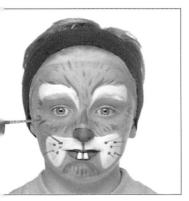

Mix a little black face paint into the purple to make a dark ple. Use this to paint the mouse's The best way to do this is to ke short, quick strokes with the brush. Paint the fur so it iates from around the eyes.

Alien from Outer Space

Aliens can come in many different forms. This extra-terrestrial beauty is the famous many-eyed creature from the planet Agog. This alien sees everything. Even when asleep, the extra pair of eyes on its eyelids keeps a watchful gaze. Just to be certain it misses nothing, the alien has a pair of cardboard eyes on straws attached to a headband. Creepy!

YOU WILL NEED

Hairband or hair elastics
Bowl of water and absorbent
* paper towels*
Face paints (green, white, blue,
* black, red)*
Fine and thick brushes

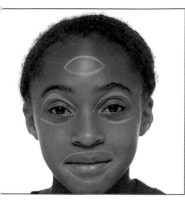

1 Tie the hair back. Use the fine brush to paint the outlines of ur oval eye shapes in green face aint. You will need to close your eyes d mouth while the outlines are ing painted.

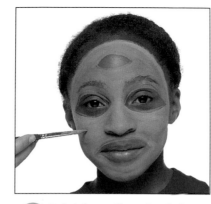

2 Paint the outline of a circle around the face in green face paint with the thick brush. Do two coats, if necessary. Fill in the outline with green. Clean and dry the thick brush thoroughly.

3 When the green face paint is dry, fill in the four eye shapes with white face paint. Do this with the clean thick brush. Apply the paint quite thickly and do two coats, if necessary.

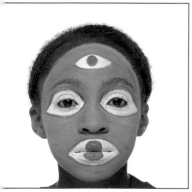

4 Let the white face paint dry thoroughly. Then paint blue rcles onto the eyes on the lips and rehead. These are the irises of the es.

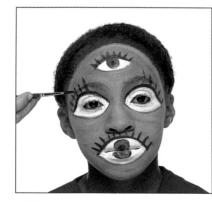

5 When the blue face paint is dry, paint a black dot onto the irises to make the pupils. Use the fine brush to paint a red line above the eyes and to make the eyelashes.

6 Close your eyes and stay very still while the irises are painted blue. When the paint is dry, paint on black pupils. Watch out! The many-eyed alien has arrived.

Happy Harlequin

A harlequin is a traditional character of mischief, magic and merriment. You can spot a harlequin by the diamond pattern on his or her costume. This harlequin is decorated not only with diamonds, but also other symbols from a pack of cards – a heart and a club. She must be the joker in the pack. Let us hope this harlequin knows some jokes that will make us laugh!

YOU WILL NEED
Hairband or hair elastics
Bowl of water and absorbent
 paper towels
Face paints (white, blue, black, red)
Round sponge
Fine and medium brushes

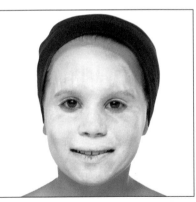

1 Tie the hair back. While the white face paint is applied to your face you should close your eyes and mouth. Apply the paint using the round sponge.

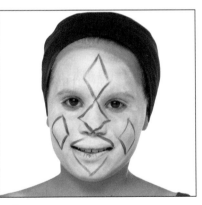

2 Let dry before painting the blue outlines of five diamonds onto the forehead, nose, cheeks and around the mouth. Do this with the fine brush.

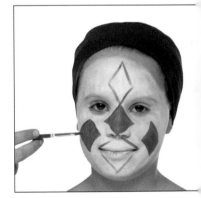

3 Fill in the two diamonds on the cheeks and the one on the nose with blue face paint using the medium brush. Let dry before doing a second coat, if necessary.

HANDY HINT

To keep hands from smudging face paints during painting, place a paper towel gently against the face. Rest your hand on the towel while you work.

4 Paint the outlines of a black club and a red heart onto the forehead using the fine brush. Fill in the outlines with black and red face paints.

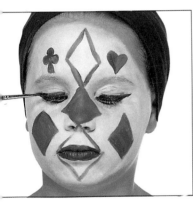

5 Close your eyes while a black line is painted onto each eyelid. Keep your eyes closed while the face paint dries. Paint the lips red using the fine brush.

Pirate of the High Seas

Welcome aboard landlubbers, and meet one of the nastiest villains that ever sailed the high seas. This pesky, painted pirate has an eye patch, curly moustache, pointy goatee and Jolly Roger tattoo. He also has a pink nose. Is this from drinking too much sea rum or from not wearing sun block?

YOU WILL NEED

Hairband or hair elastics
Bowl of water and absorbent
  paper towels
Face paints (black, green, red,
  pink, purple)
Fine and medium brushes
Natural sponge

1 Tie the hair back. Use black face paint and the fine brush to paint the moustache. It is a good idea to start at the center of the upper lip and work outward. You will have to stay still while this is being done.

2 Paint the outline for the eye patch with the fine brush. Close your eye while the outline is filled with black face paint. Paint a bushy eyebrow. Clean the brush and paint the green straps for the eye patch.

3 Clean the fine brush. Paint the skull and crossbones tattoo with red face paint. Do this detail work with the fine brush. Remember to leave the eyes and the mouth of the skull unpainted.

4 Paint on the pointy goatee using black face paint and the medium brush. Do not make the goatee too neat – pirates are a disheveled bunch.

5 Use the natural sponge to gently dab the nose with pink face paint. Then dab purple face paint over the top of the pink. Blend the colors at the edges.

HANDY HINT

A pirate's costume is easy to put together. All you need is a plain or striped T-shirt, a pair of baggy pants, a sword and a head scarf. Decorate the scarf with a Jolly Roger cut from white paper and glued to the scarf. All pirates need rope so they can swing onto other ships and steal the loot!

The Vampire

When it comes to being truly scary, vampires know all the tricks. They dress in black and only come out at night. Their faces are creepy. Who else would dare to be seen with drooling fangs and red-rimmed eyes?

YOU WILL NEED

Hairband or hair elastics
Bowl of water and absorbent paper towels
Face paints (white, black, red)
Round and natural sponges
Fine and medium brushes
Red and black make-up pencils or face crayons

1 Tie the hair back. Close your eyes and mouth while a light coat of white face paint is applied with the round sponge. Let dry.

2 Paint outlines in black for the dark areas on the forehead, cheeks and chin. Fill these areas with black using the medium brush.

3 Use the fine brush to paint the heavy eyebrows in black face paint. Let dry before doing a second coat, if necessary.

4 Close your eyes while a white line is painted on both eyelids. When dry, use the natural sponge to dab black shadows below the eyebrows and around the jawline and forehead. Draw a red line under the eyes.

5 Color the lips black with a black make-up pencil or face crayon. The vampire should smile while this is being done so the lip color goes on smoothly, but do vampires ever smile?

6 Outline the drooling fangs with black face paint using the fine brush. Now for the final gory touch. Use a clean brush to dab a little red face paint onto the ends of the fangs and just below the eyes. Gross!

Wicked Witch

Witches are an essential part of the Halloween tradition. This witch is a horrible shade of green – maybe she ate someone gross. She has a wrinkled face and lots of hairy warts. No wonder she does not look happy! To feel right at home in the role of a witch, why not make a broomstick from long twigs and have a spider for a pet?

YOU WILL NEED

Hairband or hair elastics
Bowl of water and absorbent paper towels
Face paints (purple, green, white, blue, red, black)
Triangular and round sponges
Fine and medium brushes

  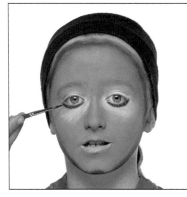

1 Tie the hair back. Use the triangular sponge to make a purple outline around the face. Fill the outline with green face paint using the round sponge. Blend the colors with the round sponge.

2 Before the green face paint dries, use the medium brush to paint some white above and below the eyes. Dab this quickly with the round sponge so it will mix with the base color.

3 Mix white and blue face paints to make light blue. Paint the lower lip light blue using the medium brush. Look up toward the ceiling and keep your head still while a red line is painted under both eyes.

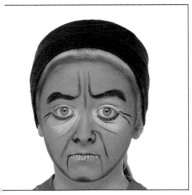 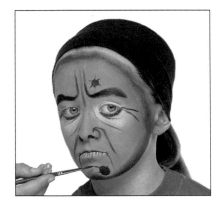 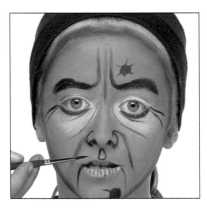

4 Use the fine and medium brushes to paint black bushy eyebrows and wrinkles. Paint creases the lips. Witches rarely smile, which is why they have deep frown es around their eyes and mouth.

5 Use the tip of the fine brush to paint red circles on the chin and forehead. Clean the brush before outlining the circles in black. Then paint black hairs sprouting from the warts.

6 Use the fine brush and black face paint to accentuate the lines under the nose. Add other nasty and gruesome details to the face, or paint the witch's hands to look old and withered.

Disco Diva

To dazzle all the other dancers at the disco, add a sparkle or two to your face with glitter gel make-up. This make-up is easy to use, but it can be messy.

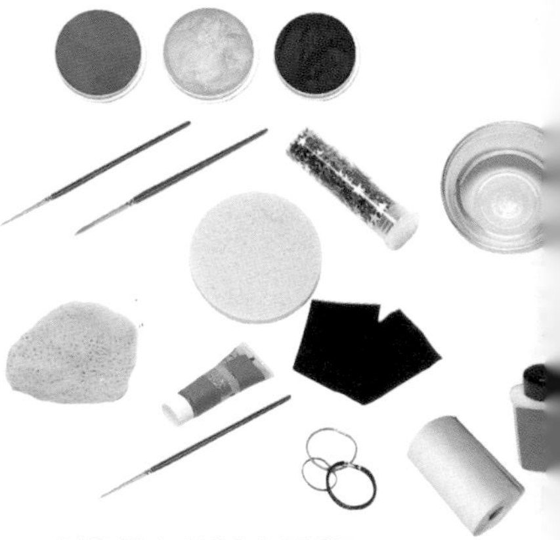

YOU WILL NEED

Hairband or hair elastics
Bowl of water and absorbent
  paper towels
Face paints (pink, turquoise,
  black)
Round and natural sponges
Fine and thick brushes
Gold glitter gel make-up and brush
Shiny stars
Face cleanser

HANDY HINT

The shiny stars can be glued to the face using special make-up glue, bu they will also stick onto the gold glitter gel make-up.

1 Tie the hair back. Apply a wide circle of pink face paint round the edge of the face using e round sponge. Do not worry if e circle is not perfect. Neaten the ges with the fine brush.

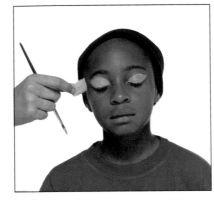

2 Paint a turquoise line with the fine brush from the inside corner of each eye up to the end of each eyebrow. Fill in with turquoise using the thick brush. Blend in the color with a damp natural sponge.

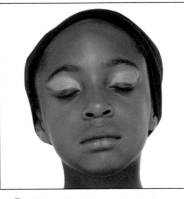

3 When the face paint is dry, paint two thin black lines onto the eyelids, as shown. Start the line from the inside corner of each eye and move outward. Keep your eyes closed until the paint has dried.

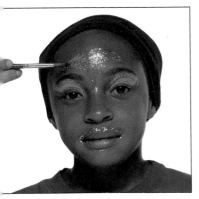

4 Use the glitter gel brush to paint the gold glitter gel onto he forehead, nose, eyelids and round the mouth. Glitter gel is uite runny, so apply it sparingly nd carefully.

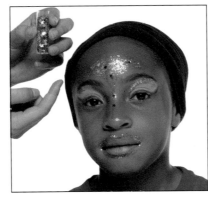

5 While the glitter gel is wet, gently press some stars onto the gel. Do not apply lots of stars in one place; they will fall off. If the gel dries before the stars are in place, paint on some more gel.

6 Stretch your lips into a broad smile while bright pink face paint is applied to your lips with the thick brush. You have every reason to smile, Disco Diva, because you are ready to go dancing!

Horrible Monster

Have you ever seen anything that looks as mean as this monster from the Black Lagoon? If not, count yourself lucky. This monster has awesome fangs and a long red tongue that just cannot help but hang out over its lips.

YOU WILL NEED

Hairband or hair elastics
Bowl of water and absorbent
* paper towels*
Face paints (purple, white,
* green, red, black, yellow)*
Medium and thick brushes
Round sponge

46

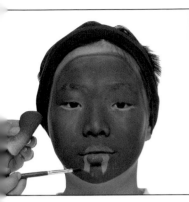

1 Tie the hair back. Paint the outline of a circle around the [fa]ce in purple face paint with the [th]ick brush. Close your eyes and [m]outh while the outline is filled in [w]ith purple using the round sponge. [L]eave gaps for the fangs.

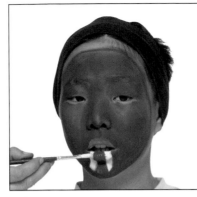

2 Let the purple base coat dry before painting the fangs white. Do two coats to make the fangs really white.

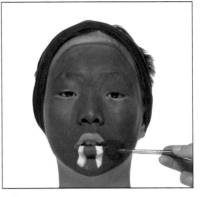

3 Smile while your upper lip is being painted green using the medium brush. Clean the brush before painting a red tongue.

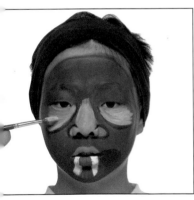

4 Paint black lines under the eyes and around the nose, as shown, [u]sing the thick brush. Clean the [b]rush. Use the clean brush to paint [t]he area above the lines yellow.

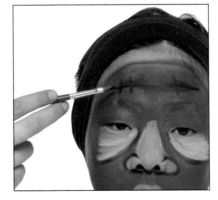

5 Use the thick brush to paint a red scar across the forehead. Paint a black line along the center of the scar. Then paint short lines across the scar to make the stitches.

6 Outline the tongue with black face paint using the medium brush. Use the same brush to paint black lines onto the upper lip. These are to make the lip look cracked.

Surprise Present

Ask a friend to paint your face as a beautifully wrapped present for a costume or Christmas party. It would also make a friend's or relative's birthday very special indeed. When choosing the colors for your face painting make sure that the painted ribbons and bow across your face really stand out. All that is missing is a gift tag that says "Surprise!"

YOU WILL NEED

Hairband or hair elastics
Bowl of water and absorbent
  paper towels, face cleanser
Face paints (blue, yellow, pink, red)
Fine and thick brushes
Gold glitter gel make-up and brush

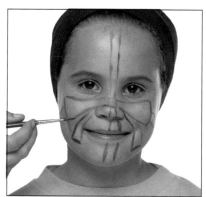

1 Tie the hair back. Use the fine brush to paint the outlines of the ribbons and bow onto the face. Paint the lines using blue face paint.

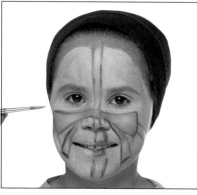

2 Let the blue paint dry. Then paint the rest of the face yellow using the thick brush. You will have to sit still while this is being done.

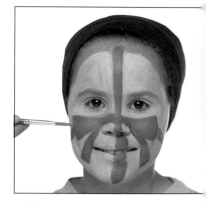

3 Clean the brush. Use the thick brush to paint the ribbon pink. Do two coats. Let the first coat dry before applying the second.

48

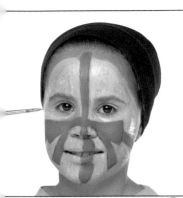

 Paint gold glitter gel make-up over the ~~low~~ base coat using ~~th~~e glitter gel brush. Let ~~dr~~y before starting the ~~ne~~xt step.

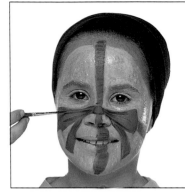

5 Paint small red lines onto the ribbon to highlight the folds and to make shadows. Do this with the fine brush.

49

Father Christmas

Ho, ho, ho, it is Christmas, so why not have your face painted as Father Christmas? Imagine how excited younger brothers or sisters would be if Santa came to spend Christmas morning with them! This Santa has a fantastic white beard and bushy eyebrows. His nose is red because it is very cold flying around the world in an open-top sleigh.

YOU WILL NEED
Hairband or hair elastics
Bowl of water and absorbent
* paper towels*
Face paints (white, black, red, pink)
Fine, medium and thick brushes

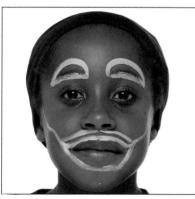

1 Tie the hair back. Paint the outlines for the eyebrows, beard and moustache, as shown. Use white face paint and the medium brush.

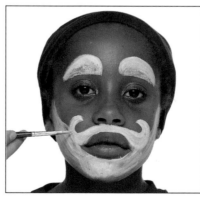

2 Fill in the outlines with white using the thick brush. To make the white really stand out, do two coats. Let the face paint dry between the first and second coats.

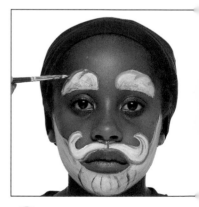

3 Mix black face paint with a little white to make gray. Use this to outline the white areas and to paint details, as shown. Use the fine brush to do this.

Use red or bright pink face paint to give Father Christmas ~wing cheeks and nose. Paint the ~tlines first using the fine brush. ~1 in the outlines using the thick ~ush. Do two coats, if necessary.

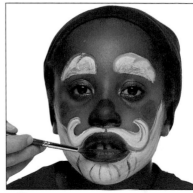

Now for the final touch. Father Christmas would not be complete without red lips. So smile, Father Christmas, while your lips are being painted. Let the paint dry before you start "Ho, ho, ho-ing!"

HANDY HINT

Put on any sweaters or T-shirts you will need for your costume before you have your face painted. If you try to pull tight clothing down over your painted face, the paint will smudge.

51

Carnival Princess

Venice, in Italy, is the home of one of the world's most famous carnivals. People wearing fantastic make-up, masks and costumes gather in Venice's narrow streets. A popular theme for many outfits is the sun. To join the carnival all you need are some shiny face paints and glitter gel make-up.

YOU WILL NEED
Hairband or hair elastics
Bowl of water and
*   absorbent paper towels*
Face paints (gold,
*   red, silver)*
Gold glitter gel make-up
*   and brush*
Round sponge
Fine brush
Face cleanser

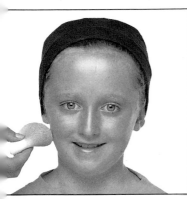

1 Tie the hair back. Apply gold face paint using the round sponge. Gold face paint is more moist than other colors, so the sponge does not have to be damp.

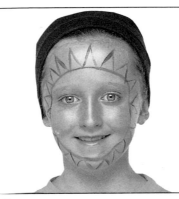

2 Let the gold face paint dry. Paint lines on the face, as shown, with red face paint, using the fine brush. The lines are the face of the sun and its rays.

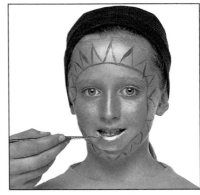

3 Make a smile while your lips are being painted with silver face paint. Do this with the fine brush. To make the lips really shine, do two coats.

4 Use the glitter gel brush to paint gold glitter gel inside the rays of the sun. Then paint the cheeks with glitter gel. Let dry before continuing.

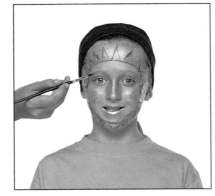

5 Paint above the eyebrows and along the bridge of the nose with gold glitter gel. To remove glitter gel make-up, use a strong face cleanser.

HANDY HINT

When using glitter gel, always protect clothing and the work surface. Use old towels or absorbent paper towels to dry hands and brushes. Do not buy ordinary glitter at a stationery store and try to glue it onto your face with paper or craft glue. Glitter gel make-up has been specially made so it will not irritate the skin.

Fake Tattoo

A tattoo is really simple and quick to do when it is done with face paint. Better still, it will wash off with soap and water. Tattoos can be painted anywhere on your body. This tattoo consists of a banner, a heart and someone's initials. You can be more adventurous and design a tattoo with animals, flowers, cars, ships or even your favorite pair of roller blades.

YOU WILL NEED
*Bowl of water and absorbent
   paper towels
Face paints (purple or black,
   red, green)
Fine and thick brushes*

1 Cover the table with paper towels. Paint the outline of the tattoo in purple or black using the fine brush.

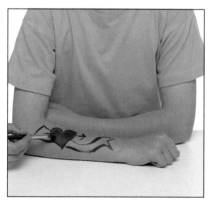

2 Let the outline dry before painting the heart red. Do this with the thick brush.

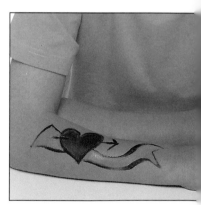

3 Clean the thick brush before using it to paint the banner green. Do two coats, if necessary.

4 Paint the initials in purple or black face paint using the fine brush. Clean the fine brush.

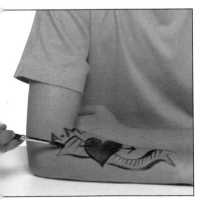

5 Decorate the banner with thin red stripes. Do this with the fine brush.

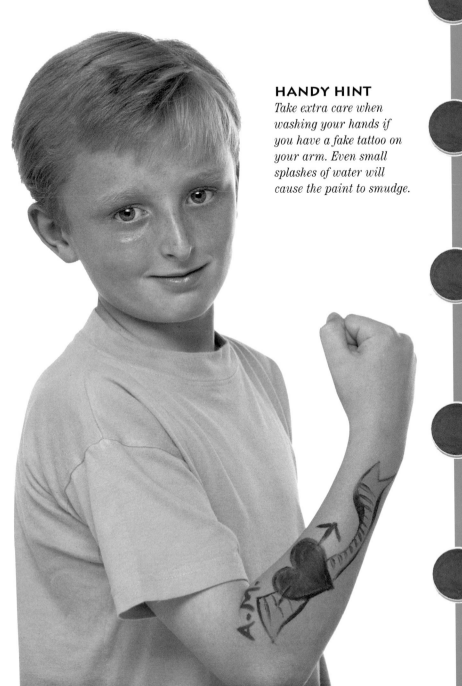

HANDY HINT

Take extra care when washing your hands if you have a fake tattoo on your arm. Even small splashes of water will cause the paint to smudge.

Friendly Green Frog

If you like green frogs, then hop to it because this is the face painting design for you. Frogs have wide mouths and catch insects with their long tongues. So to be an authentic frog you will have to stick your tongue way, way out! Do not forget to go "Croak, croak."

YOU WILL NEED
Hairband or hair elastics
Bowl of water and absorbent paper towels

Face paints (green, yellow, red, orange, black)
Fine and medium brushes
Round and natural sponges

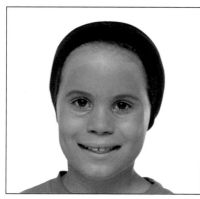

1 Tie the hair back. Paint a circle around each eye and then paint a large circle around the face. Do this with green face paint and the medium brush. Fill in the large circle using the round sponge and the brush.

2 Clean the brush. Fill in the circles around the eyes with yellow face paint. Use the natural sponge to gently dab yellow face paint above and beside the mouth, as shown. The sponge will give a dappled effect.

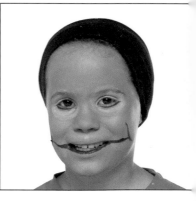

3 Paint a long red line extending from either side of the mouth. Paint the lower lip red using the medium brush. This is the frog's wide mouth. Look up and keep your head still while two red lines are being painted under your eyes.

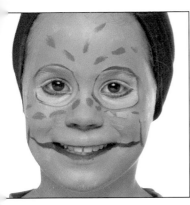

4 Clean the brush before changing colors. Paint [th]e tip of the nose orange. [Th]en paint several rows of [do]ts radiating out from the [c]enter of the face. Use the [fi]ne brush to paint black [li]nes around both eyes.

5 Use the fine brush and black face paint to paint a thin line across both eyelids, as shown. Let them dry before painting above these lines with green face paint. Do two coats. Time to find a lily pad in a shaded pond, friendly frog.

Intergalactic Robot

Be transformed into a robot with supernatural abilities. Your radar vision will let you know when enemy space ships are approaching. The reflective metal casing around your head and body will protect you during intergalactic battles. To make the costume, you will need a cereal box and aluminum foil.

YOU WILL NEED
Hairband or hair elastics
Bowl of water and absorbent paper towels
Face paints (silver, purple, blue, black)
Round sponge
Fine and medium brushes

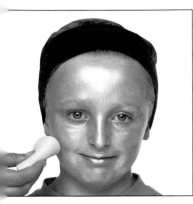
1 Tie the hair back. Close your eyes and mouth while your [fa]ce is painted with the silver face [pa]int using the round sponge.

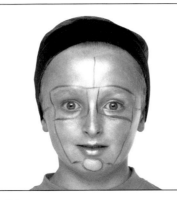
2 When the paint is dry, use the fine brush to paint purple lines onto the face. These are the panels of the reflective metal casing.

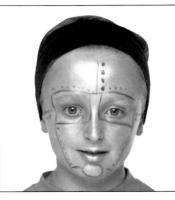
3 Paint small purple dots beside the lines using the tip of the fine brush. These are the rivets that hold the panels together.

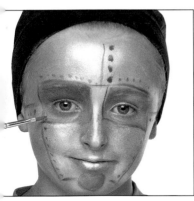
4 Paint the circle below the mouth blue using the medium [b]rush. Then paint the rectangles [a]round the eyes.

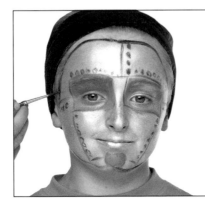
5 Clean the fine brush before starting this step. Use the fine brush to paint a black outline around the face.

HANDY HINT

Always replace the lids or screw caps onto face paints or glitter gels. This will keep them moist and clean. Wash and dry your face-painting tools when you are finished. Pack the brushes carefully so the bristles remain straight.

Egyptian Queen

The mummified bodies of Egyptian kings and queens were encased in beautiful gold and jeweled caskets. These caskets were often painted with the image of the dead person. This face painting of an Egyptian queen was inspired by one of those images. To make the headdress, cut out and decorate a piece of black cardboard.

YOU WILL NEED
Hairband or hair elastics
Bowl of water and absorbent paper towels
Face paints (gold, black, turquoise, red)
Round sponge
Fine, medium and thick brushes

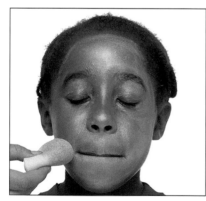

1 Tie the hair back. Close your eyes and mouth while your face is painted with gold using the round sponge. Let the gold face paint dry thoroughly.

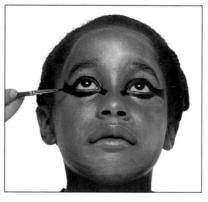

2 Close your eyes so thick black lines can be painted above both eyes. Keep your eyes closed until the paint has dried. Paint black lines under the eyes.

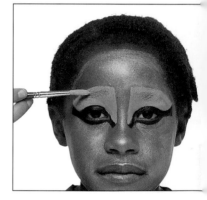

3 When dry, paint two turquoise lines from the nose to the eyebrows. Then paint lines following the curve of the eyebrows using the thick brush. Fill in the outlines.

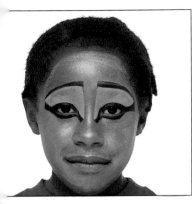

4 Let the paint dry before painting black lines above the ebrows, as shown. Use a clean fine ush to do this.

5 It is time for you to smile, your majesty, while your lips are eing painted red with the medium rush. All bow to the Queen of he Nile.

Ghostly Ghoul

Ghouls are spirits that haunt cemeteries. These vaporous beings are able to take on many disguises. You, too, can change the way you look with face painting. To be a truly one-of-a-kind ghoul, you are going to transform yourself into a crying ghoul. Instead of going "Boo!" this ghoul goes "Boo, hoo!" To complete your spooky transformation all you need is a white sheet.

YOU WILL NEED
Hairband or hair elastics
Bowl of water and absorbent
* paper towels*
Face paints (white, purple,
* green, black, blue)*
Fine, medium and thick brushes

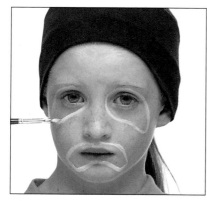

1 Tie the hair back. Paint a white frown around the mouth using the medium brush. Then paint a white circle around both eyes.

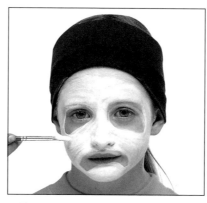

2 Close your eyes and mouth while your face is painted with white face paint using the thick brush. Do not paint inside the circles or the frown. Let dry.

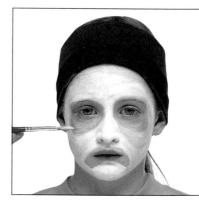

3 Mix together purple and white face paint to make pale purple. Use the thick brush to paint this around the eyes, as shown. Blend this color into the white base coat.

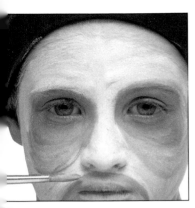

1 Clean the thick brush. Combine green and white face paint to make a very pale green. Paint this color around the mouth using the thick brush. Try to make the edges as even as possible.

5 Make sure the pale purple face paint is dry before starting this step. Paint black lines under the eyes using the fine brush. Use the thick brush to paint a blue tear on the ghoul's cheek.

ACKNOWLEDGMENTS

The Publishers would like to thank the following children for modeling for this book –

Maria Bloodworth
Liam Green
Lauren Celeste Hooper
Mitzi Johanna Hooper
Yew-Hong Mo
Jessica Moxley
Aiden Mulcahy
Fiona Mulcahy
Alexandra Richards
Leigh Richards
Frankie David Viner
Sophie Louise Viner

Gratitude also to their parents and to the Walnut Tree Walk Primary School.